Contents

Chapter 1
The Twins

Some twins are hard to tell apart. Ben and Clare weren't those sort of twins. Ben had freckles, Clare didn't. Ben had fair hair, Clare had brown hair. Clare liked to paint her nails pink, Ben didn't. It was easy to tell the twins apart.

Their mum often said they were like chalk and cheese. Clare thought Ben was the cheese.

The twins were like most brothers and sisters. Sometimes they played together and sometimes they argued. But there was one thing they agreed upon – competitions. They were both crazy about competitions.

It was amazing where you could find competitions if you looked. They were in magazines and comics.

They were on cereal packets, tubes of toothpaste and bags of crisps.

Ben and Clare often entered six or seven competitions in one week.

Ben said that if you entered enough competitions, some day you had to win. It was only a matter of time.

And as it turned out, he was right.

Chapter 2
Sweet Dreams

One Saturday afternoon, the twins were sitting in the kitchen. They had a big pile of competitions in front of them. At that moment, they were puzzling over a competition to win a shiny red sports car. (The twins couldn't drive, but they thought it would be fun to learn.)

Their mum came over to the table and dropped two Wibble's chocolate bars in front of them. "There we are," she said. "To help you think."

"Thanks, Mum!" cried the twins. Both of them grabbed the chocolate bars at the same time. They started to tear them open.

Luckily, Ben spotted something before it was too late.

"Wait!" he said. "There's some writing on this wrapper. It's a competition!"

Clare looked and saw he was right. In big red letters on the wrapper, it said:

WIN YOUR WEIGHT IN
CHOCOLATE! SEE INSIDE.

The twins stared at each other, speechless with excitement. This was the competition of their dreams.

Both of them were mad about chocolate. If they had their way, they would have had chocolate for breakfast, lunch and supper. Who needed a sports car? This was a competition they had to enter.
Each of them tried to imagine their own weight in chocolate. One thing was for sure. It would be a lot.

Carefully, Clare peeled off the wrapper and read the rules of the competition.

"In no more than ten words, say why Wibble's chocolate is the best," she read.

"That's easy," said Ben. "It's yummy. That's only two words."

Clare wrinkled her nose. "It's got to be clever, Ben. You can't just say 'it's yummy'. Anyway, 'scrummy' sounds better."

"Okay, it's yummy and scrummy," said Ben.

"That's good, it rhymes," said Clare. "Wait a minute." She chewed on her pencil, thinking.

"It's yummy and scrummy ... And it's going in my tummy," she laughed.

That sounded good. They wrote it down on the entry form.

Wibble's Chocolate is the best:
because it's yummy and scrummy... And it's going in my tummy.

"Ten words exactly," counted Clare. "Perfect."

Next, you had to write your name and address and your weight.

Usually, they took turns to enter their names for a competition. Ben said it was his turn.

"No," argued Clare. "Your name was going on the sports car competition. So it's my turn."

"I don't want it on that. I want my name on this one," said Ben, stubbornly.

"All right. I know how to decide,"
said Clare. She gave a sly smile. "We'll
see who is the heaviest."

"What's that got to do with it?"
asked Ben.

"It's obvious, noodle," said Clare.

"You win your weight in chocolate.
So the more you weigh, the more
chocolate you get!"

"Oh," said Ben. "I never thought of
that."

They both raced upstairs to the bathroom. Ben got there first and jumped on the scales. He weighed 22 kilos. But when Clare stood on the scales she weighed 25 kilos.

"Cheater! You knew that all along," said Ben.

Clare just pulled a face. In the end, it was her name and weight that went on the entry form.

Chapter 3
Always a Chance

They sealed up the envelope and took it to the post box.

"I'll post it," said Ben.

"Let's both post it," said Clare. "Maybe it will bring us luck."

They both took one corner of the envelope and pushed it into the slot.

"Do you think we'll win?" Ben asked.

"There's always a chance," said Clare.

They'd said that lots of times before. They'd entered hundreds of competitions. But they'd never won anything, except a measly set of felt-tip pens.

"Say we did win," said Ben. "We'd share the prize, wouldn't we? I mean, we've entered together."

"Of course," said Clare. But as she said it, for some reason, she crossed her fingers behind her back.

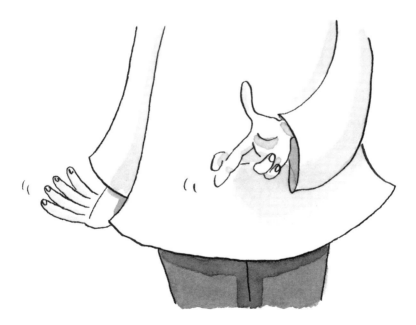

Chapter 4
Lucky You

The weeks went by, and the twins forgot all about the Wibble's chocolate bar competition. Then, one Friday evening, the doorbell rang.

Ben opened the door to find a smartly dressed woman outside. Behind her, stood a man with a camera.

The woman gave Ben a friendly smile.

"Hello. Does Clare Mimms live here?" she asked.

"Yes," said Ben. "She's my sister."

"Lucky you," said the smiling woman. "Can you get her for me? She's won a prize."

It took Ben about three seconds flat to dash upstairs and fetch Clare.

His mind was racing. He tried to remember which competitions they'd entered recently. What kind of prize had Clare won?

Mum joined them at the door to see what was happening.

"My name's Diane. I'm from Wibble ..." the smart lady began.

"Wibble?" said Clare. "The chocolate makers?"

"Yes, and I'm delighted to say you've won our competition, Clare. We loved your slogan. How did it go? *It's yummy and scrummy —*"

"— *And it's going in my tummy!*" shouted Ben and Clare together.

"That was it," said Diane. "Now, if you'd all stand back, we'll bring your prize in."

A large, red Wibble's chocolate van stood outside their house. Two men were unloading something from the back.

It was the biggest chocolate bar the
twins had ever seen. It was huge,
immense – almost as big as a door.
The giant Wibble bar was wrapped in
shiny red paper. The delivery men
wheeled it into the house on a trolley.

"Oh, my goodness!" said Mum, goggling at the whopper bar.

"It's bigger than me!" shouted Ben.

"I won! I won! I won!" shouted Clare, dancing round the room.

"It weighs 25 kilos. Exactly your weight, Clare," said Diane. "If you'll just stand next to it, we'll take a photo for the newspaper."

Clare stood with one arm round her prize and a huge grin on her face. Ben felt he should have been in the photo, too.

But he wasn't asked.

At last, everyone went away and the three of them were left alone. Clare put the giant Wibble bar on the sofa.

They all looked at it. No one spoke
for a while.

"Well! What are you going to do
with it?" asked their mum at last.

"That's easy," grinned Ben. "We're
going to eat it. Aren't we, Clare?"

Clare said nothing.

Chapter 5
You Promised!

After supper, Clare counted the squares of the chocolate bar. She felt them through the wrapper. There were seventy-two. Clare worked out that would last her about ten weeks if she ate one square a day.

Of course, if she shared the bar with Ben, it would only last five weeks. That was the trouble. She wasn't sure that she wanted to share her prize.

"Let's have a piece," said Ben, eagerly.

"No," said Clare. She wasn't ready to tear open the shiny red wrapper. It looked too perfect.

That was the trouble with Ben. He would never save anything. He'd rip off all the paper right away. Then he'd stuff himself with so much chocolate that he'd probably be sick.

"It's not up to you," said Ben.

"It is," replied Clare. "It's *my* prize."

"It's mine as well," said Ben. "It's *our* prize. You promised to share."

"Maybe I've changed my mind," said Clare. She hadn't meant to say that. It had just come out. She knew she wasn't being fair but Ben was starting to annoy her.

This was her prize. The only prize she'd ever won in her life. She wasn't going to let her brother spoil it.

Ben screwed up his face like a baby.

"That's not fair! You promised!" he shouted.

"If you must know, I had my fingers crossed. So it doesn't count," replied Clare. "Anyway, it's got my name on the label."

"It could just as easy be mine," argued Ben.

"But it *isn't*," hissed Clare. "It's *my* prize and they gave it to *me*. I can do what I like with it."

She grabbed the giant bar and dragged it out of the room.

"I'll get you back for this!" Ben yelled after her.

It took a lot of effort to get the bar upstairs and into her bedroom, but, in the end, Clare managed it.

Chapter 6
The Hiding Place

Clare didn't come out of her room all evening. She laid the giant Wibble bar on the floor. She was feeling a bit guilty about Ben.

Maybe she ought to give in and let him have a piece of her chocolate? But that meant tearing open the shiny wrapper.

Clare wasn't ready to do that yet.

She liked to save her sweets for the right moment.

Later, she told herself, she would let Ben have a piece. Later, but not yet. If she ate just one small piece a day, she could make it last for a long, long time.

Ben, meanwhile, was sulking in his room. He wasn't speaking to his sister.

When he met Clare going into the bathroom, he glared at her silently.

Clare brushed her teeth and got ready for bed.

She went to sleep with the giant
Wibble bar on the floor next to her
bed.

In the middle of the night, she woke
up. She'd been having a terrible
nightmare.

In her dream, Ben sneaked into her
room while she was asleep. Then he
ate all the chocolate.

"I told you I'd get you back," he smiled, with chocolate smeared all round his mouth.

Clare woke up in a cold panic.

She switched on her bedside lamp. To her relief, the giant Wibble bar was still on the floor, unopened.

She got out of bed and picked it up. After her nightmare, she wanted to hide her prize in a safe place.

She opened up her wardrobe. The
wardrobe was jammed with clothes
and shoes. There wasn't room for a
kingsize chocolate bar.

Clare sat down on her bed. She
looked around the room. Between her
bed and the wall, she saw a narrow
gap. It looked just wide enough to hide
a giant chocolate bar.

When she tried it, the bar slid
neatly into the gap. It was wedged
between the bed and the radiator.
Perfect.

Once Clare had replaced her duvet, you wouldn't know that anything was there.

Back in bed, she smiled to herself. Her treasure was safe. Ben would never think of looking in her secret hiding place.

Chapter 7
A Nasty Feeling

In the morning, Clare woke up. She looked on the floor. Then she remembered where she'd hidden the giant bar last night. She felt hungry. Should she have some now, or save it until after school?

Perhaps she'd just steal the tiniest piece now. To see what it tasted like.

Downstairs, she could hear her mum and her brother in the kitchen.

It was safe to get the bar out. The more she thought about the chocolate, the more she longed to taste it.

She imagined peeling back the red wrapper. She imagined the snap the chocolate would make when she broke off the first piece. Would it taste like ordinary milk chocolate? Or would it be better? Sweeter and creamier?

Clare felt down the side of the bed with her hand.

Instead of the large solid bar, her hand touched the hot radiator. A horrible thought crossed her mind.

She leapt out of bed. Her bare feet felt sticky. Looking down, she saw the carpet was swimming in something thick and brown. There was a strong, sweet smell in the room. A smell like ... like melted chocolate!

Clare got down on her hands and knees and felt under the bed. Her hand came out coated with a brown gooey mess. Under the bed, she could see the bar's shiny red wrapper, crumpled and empty. Chocolate ran down the radiator and oozed in brown waves across the floor.

"No!" Clare wailed. "My beautiful prize! Oh, no, NO!"

Mum and Ben heard her cries and ran upstairs. When they burst into the room, Clare was still on her hands and knees. She was trying to scoop the melted chocolate back into its wrapper.

"Clare! What's the matter? Are you all right?" asked her mum.

"Ugh!" said Ben. "What's all this stuff on the floor?"

"My chocolate bar!" moaned Clare. "It melted on the radiator!"

"What?" said her mum. She looked down in horror at the carpet swimming in chocolate. "Clare, what on earth made you leave it by a hot radiator?"

"It wasn't hot last night," whined Clare. "I just wanted to hide it from Ben."

Ben looked down at his sister. She had chocolate all over her pyjamas, chocolate sticking to her fingers, chocolate in her hair and a big blob on the end of her nose.

He burst out laughing. "I thought you wanted to eat it," he grinned. "Not wear it!"

Later that day, Clare knocked on Ben's bedroom door. Ben was on his bed, reading a comic. He didn't look up.

Clare took something out of her pocket. She dropped it into his lap. It was a chocolate bar – a Wibble's chocolate bar.

"I know it's not the same," said
Clare. "But I just wanted to say sorry."

Ben slowly tore off the wrapper.

"I suppose we could always share
it," he said.

Clare smiled, but Ben wasn't
looking. He was staring at the
wrapper.

"Wait a minute," he said. "There's
another competition on here!"

About the author

I live in Nottingham and write children's books and scripts for television.

Yummy Scrummy started from reading about "compers" – people who enter competitions all the time. It was the idea of winning your weight in chocolate that really appealed to me.

Do you think you'd be like Clare, or would you share the prize?